Pebble® Plus

PIRATES AHOY!

Pirate Gear

by Rosalyn Tucker

Consulting editor: Gail Saunders-Smith, PhD

CAPSTONE PRESS
a capstone imprint

Pebble Plus is published by Capstone Press,
1710 Roe Crest Drive, North Mankato, Minnesota 56003
www.capstonepub.com

Library of Congress Cataloging-in-Publication Data

24.65

Tucker, Rosalyn.
Pirate gear / by Rosalyn Tucker.
pages cm. — (Pebble plus. pirates ahoy!)
Includes bibliographical references and index.
ISBN 978-1-4914-2112-3 (library binding)
ISBN 978-1-4914-2353-0 (eBook PDF)
1. Pirates—Juvenile literature. I. Title.
G535.T774 2015
910.4'5—dc23   2014023827.

Editorial Credits

Michelle Hasselius, editor; Kazuko Collins, designer; Pam Mitsakos, media researcher; Gene Bentdahl, production specialist

Photo Credits

Alamy: © Mary Evans Picture Library, 5, © Wim Wiskerke, 15; Bridgeman Images: Look and Learn, 11, 13, 17, cover; Mary Evans Picture Library: 19; Shutterstock: Dmitrijs Bindemanis, 21, Elenarts, 7, Eva Bidiuk (ship silhouette), cover, Triff, 9
Design Elements: Shutterstock: A-R-T (old paper), La Gorda (rope illustration), vovan (old wood)

Note to Parents and Teachers

The Pirates Ahoy! set supports national curriculum standards for social studies related to people, places, and environments. This book describes and illustrates pirate gear. The images support early readers in understanding the text. The repetition of words and phrases helps early readers learn new words. This book also introduces early readers to subject-specific vocabulary words, which are defined in the Glossary section. Early readers may need assistance to read some words and to use the Table of Contents, Glossary, Read More, Internet Sites, and Index sections of the book.

Printed in China by Nordica.
0914/CA21401504
092014   008470NORDS15

Table of Contents

Living at Sea

Pirates lived at sea during the
Golden Age of Piracy (1690–1730).
Pirates needed a lot of gear
to live and fight on pirate ships.

Pirates could spend months at sea.

Sailing Tools

Sails were like engines for ships. Pirates raised sails high into the air on masts. The sails caught strong winds. The wind pushed the ships through the water.

sails

The more sails a ship had, the faster it could go.

Pirates needed special gear to guide their ships. They used maps, charts, and compasses to find their way. Pirates often stole these items from other ships.

A compass helped a pirate sail in the right direction.

Battle Gear

Pirates always had to be ready to
fight. Cannons were powerful weapons
on a ship. Pirates also fought with
short swords called cutlasses.

Large ships could carry more than 40 cannons.

Pirates threw stinkpots onto a ship before they attacked. Stinkpots were clay pots filled with smelly fish parts. Pirates wanted to make the ship's crew too sick to fight.

A ship's crew was easier to fight against after pirates threw stinkpots.

One of the most useful weapons

was a pirate's Jolly Roger flag.

Pirates painted skulls or bones

on their flags to scare other sailors.

a Jolly Roger flag

Food and Fun

Pirates kept salted meats and drinking water on their ships. But sometimes they needed more food. Pirates caught fish. But they also stole fresh food from other ships.

Pirates could hunt for food
when they were on land.

Sometimes pirates got bored at sea. They played music with drums and fiddles. Some pirates even had pets such as parrots or monkeys.

Pirates are often shown with parrots in books and paintings.

Learning from Pirates

Charts, weapons, and sails were important gear for pirates. We study these tools to learn about pirate life. Pirate gear is displayed in museums today.

Pirate gear can be found in museums around the world.

Glossary

cannon—a heavy gun that fires large metal balls

compass—a tool used for finding directions

cutlass—a short sword with a curved blade

display—to show something

engine—a machine that makes the power needed to move something

fiddle—a violin

gear—items needed for a job or an activity

Golden Age of Piracy—the period from 1690 to 1730, when thousands of people became pirates around the world

mast—a tall pole on a ship's deck that holds its sails

pirate—a person who steals from ships and towns

Read More

Bunting, Eve. *P is for Pirate: A Pirate Alphabet.* Ann Arbor, Mich.: Sleeping Bear Press, 2014.

Jenson-Elliott, Cindy. *Pirates' Tools for Life at Sea.* Pirates! Mankato, Minn.: Capstone Press, 2013.

Pratt, Laura. *Pirates.* Learn to Draw. New York: AV2 by Weigl, 2013.

Internet Sites

FactHound offers a safe, fun way to find Internet sites related to this book. All of the sites on FactHound have been researched by our staff.

Here's all you do:

Visit *www.facthound.com*

Type in this code: 9781491421123

Super-cool stuff!

Check out projects, games and lots more at
www.capstonekids.com

Index

Word Count: 230

Grade: 1

Early-Intervention Level: 21